Anita Shackelford
& Jennifer Perdue

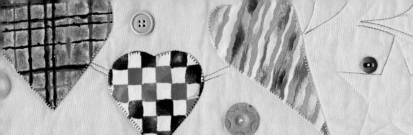

Teens & Tweens

Quilting Fun with **Family & Friends**

Located in Paducah, Kentucky, the American Quilter's Society (AQS) is dedicated to promoting the accomplishments of today's quilters. Through its publications and events, AQS strives to honor today's quiltmakers and their work and to inspire future creativity and innovation in quiltmaking.

EXECUTIVE BOOK EDITOR: ANDI MILAM REYNOLDS
GRAPHIC DESIGN: ELAINE WILSON
COVER DESIGN: MICHAEL BUCKINGHAM
PHOTOGRAPHY: CHARLES R. LYNCH, FINISHED PROJECTS
STEP-BY-STEP PHOTOGRAPHY: ANITA SHACKELFORD AND JENNIFER PERDUE; ANITA SHACKELFORD PHOTO: RICHARD SHACKELFORD

Thanks to the models Amber Perdue and Makenzie Pegram.

Additional copies of this book may be ordered from the American Quilter's Society, PO Box 3290, Paducah, KY 42002-3290, or online at www.AmericanQuilter.com.

Text © 2009, Authors, Anita Shackelford & Jennifer Perdue
Artwork © 2009, American Quilter's Society

LIBRARY OF CONGRESS CATALOGING-IN-PUBLICATION DATA

Shackelford, Anita.
  Teens and tweens quilting fun with family and friends / by Anita Shackelford and Jennifer Perdue.
    p. cm.
  ISBN 978-1-57432-996-4
  1. Machine quilting. 2. Machine quilting--Patterns. I. Perdue, Jennifer. II. Title.
  TT835.S46265 2009
  746.46'041--dc22
                                        2009023942

American Quilter's Society
P. O. Box 3290 • Paducah, KY 42002-3290
www.AmericanQuilter.com

Acknowledgments

Our first thank you goes to our group of new quilters. Thank you for sharing your time and talents on these new projects. You were creative thinkers, whether you were recycling favorite jeans and t-shirts, or making something personalized to give to a friend. It was a joy working with you, and we learned so much from you:

Rose Willow Buckelew, Kaitlin Finkler, Samantha Finkler, Beverly Morgan, Amber Perdue, Brandon Perdue, Dakota Rapp, Seayra Spears, Blake Zealor, Elisa Shackelford Zealor.

To our husbands, Richard and Scott, for their love and encouragement as we began to travel this road together. Thank you for the time we needed to be creative and to share our love of quilting with others. We love you.

To the designers who created wonderful quilting patterns to add just the right texture and style to our quilts: Tanya del Tongo Armanasco, Janice Bahrt, Todd Brown, Kim Diamond, Mary Eddy, Tammy Finkler, Ellen Munnich, Kay Oft, Paul Statler, and Marty Vint. You make the world a more beautiful place.

To Bill and Meredith Schroeder for their continuing support of today's quiltmakers and for recognizing the importance of bringing young people into this art we love.

To Andi Reynolds for understanding our vision of this book and making it all come to life.

To Elaine Wilson for the beautiful pages and capturing the creative energy of this new generation.

To Charles Lynch for his special touch in photographing our projects.

Other photograpy credits:
Tammy Finkler photo: Dennis Finkler; Girls' photos: Tammy Finkler.

Contents

Introduction

It is often said that creative arts such as sewing and quilting skip a generation.

Things go out of style and then, after a while, are rediscovered by another generation of young people. This was true in my family.

My grandmother was a quilter—a product of the Depression—when sewing was more a matter of economy than of creativity. She also made many of my clothes, so I was exposed to sewing as I was growing up.

My mother did not sew. She went directly from high school to factory work during WWII. In the 1950s, part of the culture shaping the "modern" housewife was that life was good and everyone was able to buy new things. No one was interested in "home-made." Hers was the generation that missed out on creating things for themselves.

I remember working with fabric from an early age and have always enjoyed making garments, quilts, and other decorative items for my home.

There is a current push to try to involve more young people in sewing. I am fortunate that both of my girls learned to sew when they were young and still enjoy doing so. I also have grandchildren who love to design and work with fabric. They were all willing apprentices for this book!

The projects we designed range from simple to complex, and include quilting, sewing, and home dec items. We have tried to include fresh, trendy materials and manageable projects which are appealing, personalized, and practical for a young person to use.

Because most children have a shorter attention span, we focused on projects that can be completed in one or two sittings. When you are sewing with children, begin with something simple. Chances are, after that item is finished, they may be willing to invest time in a longer, more involved project.

Once young people feel the sense of satisfaction in creating something new, something for themselves or their family or friends, they will enjoy sewing forever.

Anita

How to Use This Book

We expect that most of the young people working on projects from this book will have an adult for guidance.

Our young designers ranged in age from 4 years to 17 years old. They had little or no sewing experience at the start. Whether you are working with young children or teens, you'll find all of them will bring some skills to the job. Be patient while you discover what these new quilters can do.

Young children can be involved in choosing colors and fabrics for their quilts. They can use crayons and paint sticks, cut out simple shapes with scissors, and sew on buttons and other embellishments. With guidance from an adult, they may be able to sew straight piecing lines with the sewing machine. They will find it helpful to use a double thread when they are hand sewing so the thread doesn't pull out of the needle. And if the project will allow, have them use a big needle, which will be easier to hold and will have a big eye for easy threading. Children have a short attention span but are eager for any new experience.

Tweens and teens can make decisions about colors and layout, iron their fabrics, use the rotary cutter with guidance, and use the sewing machine with instruction. They bring lots of enthusiasm and a creative eye to the work.

Older teens and young adults may find projects that will appeal to them. Those who already have good sewing skills should be able to follow the step-by-step instructions and complete a piece on their own, but having a good resource person on hand is invaluable.

Supervising adults may want to do some of the rotary cutting ahead of time to help get a project started, or as a demo for older children. Adults can also sit at the sewing machine with smaller children to watch fingers and help guide fabric. And, of course, everyone loves it when someone helps with the ironing!

Most of all, share your passion for pattern, color, fabric, sewing, quilting, and the satisfaction gained by making something yourself.

Enjoy,
Anita & Jen

Getting Ready

Every construction job needs a tool box. For each project, we've listed the big tools, smaller gear, and other supplies you'll need before you start. You may not need everything on this Master List; the items will vary from project to project, so take a look at the directions and make sure you have what you need to get the job done.

The Big Tools

Rotary cutter*, mat, and rulers (large and small)

Iron and ironing board

Sewing machine with specialty feet** for piecing, appliqué, decorative stitching***, and quilting

Longarm quilting machine (optional)

Serger (optional)

*Special blades for rotary cutters can give you wavy or scalloped edges, among others.

**Specialty feet include a ¼" foot for sewing seams; different feet for zigzag, zipper, and decorative stitches; and a walking foot for quilting.

***Some sewing machines have specialty stitches programmed into them.

Other Gear

Small scissors

Straight pins

Hand sewing needles

Masking tape (various sizes)

Measuring tape

Non-stick pressing sheet

Digital camera (optional)

Digitized embroidery or quilting patterns (optional)

Quilting stencils

Key rings

Carabiner or "D" hook

Awl and wood block

Staple gun—optional

Small wood screws 4 x ¾" and a screwdriver

Supplies

Pen and paper for notes and rubbings

Crayons or paint sticks

White or clear glue

Freezer paper

Colorful index cards

Fabric, including old jeans, special t-shirts, and other fave clothes

Clear upholstery vinyl

20" pillow form or a bag of fiberfill for stuffing

Threads—for sewing and for embellishing, including cotton, transparent, metallic, and embroidery floss

Batting

Embellishments such as buttons, ribbons, hot glue crystals, beads, and charms

Fusible web for appliqué

Projects

Accessories & Clothing

Friendship Cards

The Big Tools
✓ Sewing machine with foot for zigzag stitching

✓ Rotary cutter, mat, and small ruler

✓ Iron and ironing board

Other Gear
✓ Small scissors

✓ Hand sewing needles

✓ Non-stick pressing sheet

Supplies
✓ Novelty fabrics

✓ Fabrics for backgrounds

✓ Colorful index cards

✓ Embellishments like beads, buttons, ribbon, yarn, or charms

✓ Fusible batting

✓ Fusible web for appliqué

✓ Thread for appliqué, adding embellishments, and finishing the edges of the card

Quilted friendship cards are fun to make and cool to give as valentines, birthday cards, or Christmas cards. The quilted side lets you be creative and the paper side gives you a place to write a note to a special friend.

AMBER

BRANDON

DAKOTA

WILLOW

Hey Baby,

Here's a sweet card I made just for you.

Love you so much!

Friendship Cards

Friendship Cards

Choose a novelty print with a picture you like or something you'd like to give to a friend.

Choose a background fabric that looks good with your picture print.

We used colorful index cards for the paper side of our friendship cards. Index cards are sturdy and will give you a good place to write a note to your friend.

Choose a picture print and a background fabric.

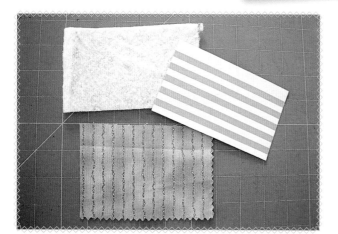

Cut a piece of background fabric a little bit bigger than the card. Cut a piece of fusible batting the same size as your background fabric.

Follow the manufacturer's directions to add fusible web behind the picture you want to use. Cut out the picture. If the picture is too small or detailed, just cut a simple shape and keep some of the background around the picture.

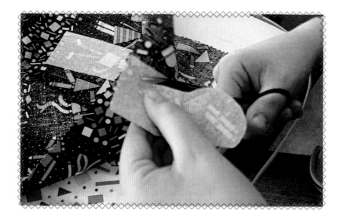

Decide where your picture looks best on the background. Peel off the paper background and use the iron to fuse the picture into place.

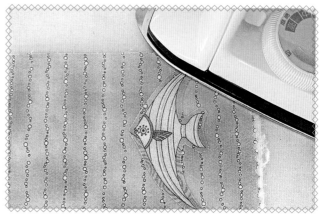

Use the sewing machine and a tiny zigzag stitch to appliqué the picture. Stitching through the background and the batting layers will add a little quilted texture.

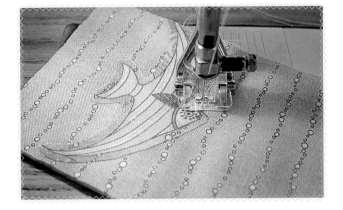

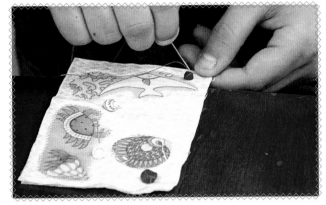

Add the embellishments by hand or machine. You can use a zigzag stitch to add yarn. Beads and buttons will be easier to sew by hand. Netting is a good way to hold other pieces in place. You can stitch a small piece of netting, like a window pane, over small embellishments, or stitch a layer of netting across the whole card.

Put the index card on the back of the little quilt you've just made. If you have dimensional embellishments, you will have to stitch with the quilt right-side up. Masking tape over the edges will help hold all of the layers together while you stitch. Be sure to remove the pieces of tape, one at a time, before you stitch that spot.

If the quilted side is flat, it will be easier to stitch the edges with the quilted side down. When you put the two pieces together under the needle, make sure the quilt is facing down and the right side of the card is up.

Using a zigzag stitch and following the edges of the card, stitch the two pieces together. Trim away any extra fabric on the edges, but be careful not to cut your stitches.

Sunglasses Case
or
Cell Phone Holder

The Big Tools
✓ Sewing machine with a zipper foot

Other Gear
✓ Scissors
✓ Pins
✓ Key ring
✓ Carabiner or "D" hook
✓ Awl and wood block

Supplies
✓ Old pair of jeans
✓ Thread to match the denim or pants fabric
✓ Heat-set crystals for embellishment (optional)

That pocket u made 4 ur glasses is so cute! Whenever we hang next I will bring my beads over. C ya then.

Take apart an old pair of jeans and recycle the pocket into a holder for your sunglasses, music player, or cell phone. Any jeans or pants pocket will work for this easy project.

Cut a back pocket from the jeans, including ½" of extra material all around. Fold the pocket in half and line up the edges of the pocket on the front and the back. Pin the layers together.

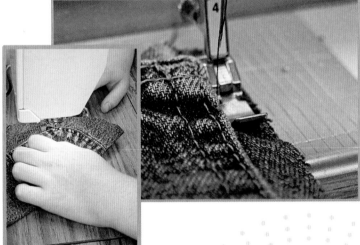

Use a zipper foot to stitch close to the pocket, down the side, and around the bottom. Stitch twice for security, backstitching at the beginning and at the end of the seam.

Amber uses the sewing machine to stitch her little pocket.

Sunglasses Case
or
Cell Phone Holder

Amber added some bling to her pocket with heat-set crystals. Using a pocket with a patch or a label would be sweet, too.

Follow the manufacturer's directions to add glue-on or heat-set crystals to your pocket, if you want some sparkle. Arrange them in any pattern you like.

We added a ring to one corner, so we can fasten the little pocket to a belt loop or back pack when we're on the move. It's cool!

Have an adult help you use an awl or other sharp tool to make a hole in the corner of the pocket. A key ring makes a good connector between the pocket and the "D" hook.

Brandon fastened his new pocket to his backpack.

Pack your stuff and get going!

Three Pocket Pouch

The Big Tools
- ✓ Sewing machine with a zipper foot and edge stitch foot, if available
- ✓ Rotary cutter, mat, and large ruler
- ✓ Iron and ironing board

Other Gear
- ✓ Scissors
- ✓ Pins
- ✓ Two key rings
- ✓ Awl and wood block

Supplies
- ✓ Old pair of jeans
- ✓ Thread to match denim
- ✓ Hook and loop patches or tape

U R 2 Cool

Three Pocket Pouch

HERE'S A GOOD WAY TO CARRY THINGS IN YOUR HIP POCKET EVEN WHEN YOU'RE NOT WEARING YOUR JEANS!

Denim goes with everything and this little pocket pouch can go everywhere with you.

Pick a pair of jeans with interesting back pockets. We liked this pair because they had colored stitching, great texture, and they were different from each other.

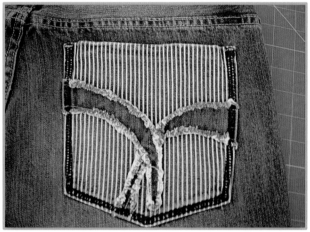

Take the jeans apart:

Cut both back pockets out of the jeans, cutting 1" extra all around. If the jeans have a seam above the pockets, include it in the piece.

Cut along an outside seam to open the leg of the jeans. Cut a strip of fabric 4" wide and as long as you can from the leg. You'll use this strip later to make the strap for your pouch.

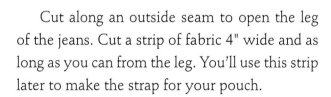

Sew the pouch together:

Place the pocket pieces wrong sides together, with both pockets showing on the outside.

Match up the pocket edges with each other front and back, and pin them together.

Put a zipper foot on your sewing machine. This narrow foot will let you stitch as close as you can to the pocket edges when you sew the two pieces together. Be sure to set the needle to the side, so it doesn't hit the zipper foot when you sew.

Sew down the side, around the bottom of the pocket, and up the other side. Stitch twice for security, backstitching at the beginning and at the end of the seam. Leave the top edge open. Trim the raw edges a little narrower, if you want to.

Make the strap:

Fold the long edges of the strap to meet in the center and then fold it in half again. Use pins to hold everything together.

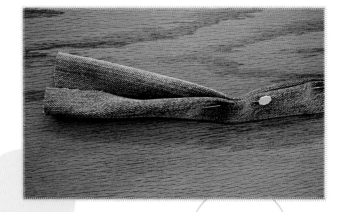

Topstitch along both long edges of the strap. Using a foot with a guide will help you sew a straight line. A decorative stitch and fancy thread might look good here.

Attach the strap:

Use an awl (see page 14) or other sharp tool to make holes in the corners of the pouch and put a key ring on each side. Pull the ends of the strap through the rings and stitch to hold them in place.

Add a fastener:

Pieces of hook and loop tape will help close the top edge so your things will stay safely tucked inside.

Your new pouch has three pockets to carry your hand-held games or other important stuff. And the best part is—you made it yourself!

DVD Carrier

The Big Tools
- ✓ Sewing machine with zigzag or other edge stitch
- ✓ Rotary cutter, mat, and large ruler

Other Gear
- ✓ Scissors
- ✓ Pins

Supplies
- ✓ Old pair of jeans
- ✓ Variegated (multicolored) thread

Hey, Dude,
I cut up my jeans last night.
Wait 'til you see what I made!

DVD Carrier • •

An old pair of jeans can be recycled to make an awesome carrier for your DVD player. Read on. You can make it in an afternoon!

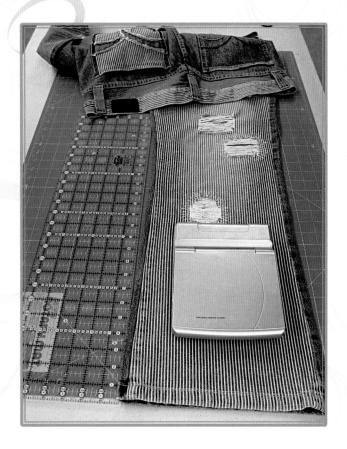

Measure the height and the width of your DVD player. You will need a jeans leg that is three times as long and 1" wider than the size of your DVD player. Measure the jeans to make sure you have enough fabric.

Example:
    DVD height 8" x 3" = 24"
    DVD width 6" + 1" = 7"

Take apart the jeans:

Cut off one leg of a pair of jeans that is as long as you need for your DVD player. Keep the hem attached. You will use both layers of the fabric (front and back of the jeans leg) at the same time.

Starting at the hem edge, measure and cut a piece of fabric 1" longer and 1" wider than the size of the player. Cut straight across, through both layers of the leg, to create the front panel.

To make the back panel and the flap, cut the rest of the jeans leg to the same width as the front panel.

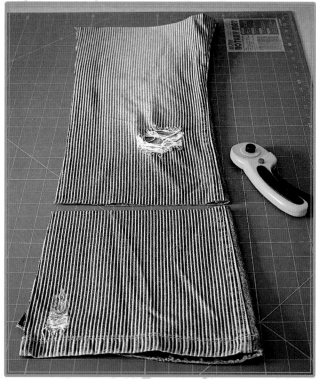

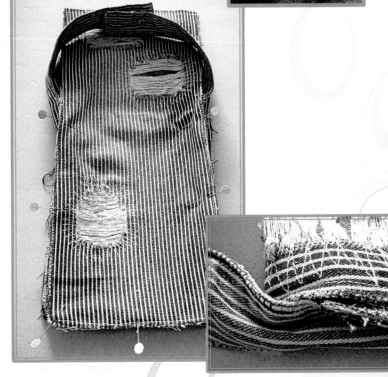

Make the strap:

Remove the waistband from the jeans. The width of the waistband should be about the same size as the depth of the player. It should fit around the player with some ease (length left over) for a handle.

Sew the strap to the front panel:

Turn the front panels so the raw edges are at the bottom. Find the center of the waistband and pin it to the center bottom (raw edges) of the front panels. Pin the other edges together and stitch around three sides of the panel, with the raw edges showing on the outside.

Cool tip: Positioning the front panel with the hem edges at the top will give you an extra pocket in the front.

Use the rest of the leg to make the back of the carrier and the flap. Keep both layers together and pin them into place, the same way you did the front. Sew the seam with the raw edges to the outside. Trim the flap to a length you like.

Finish all of the edges with a variegated thread and a blanket stitch or other fancy stitching and you will be good to go!

Laptop Cover

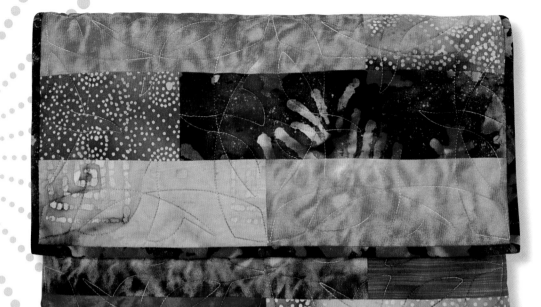

Awesome laptop cover!
Can U show me how 2 make 1?

The Big Tools
✓ Sewing machine with specialty feet for piecing and quilting
✓ Rotary cutter, mat, and small ruler
✓ Iron and ironing board

Other Gear
✓ Scissors
✓ Pins
✓ Hand sewing needles

Supplies
✓ ⅔ yard fabric for the outside
✓ ⅔ yard fabric for the lining
✓ ¼ yard fabric for the binding
✓ Batting
✓ Sewing thread
✓ Quilting thread

Make a quilted cover to fit your laptop; keep your baby safe when you're on the move.

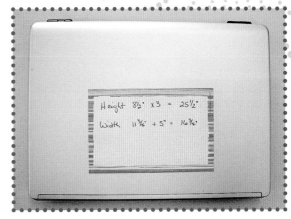

Measure the height and width of your laptop.

Multiply the height of the laptop times 3 and write down the number. Add 5" to the width of the laptop and write down that number, too.

Piece together a quilt top as big as your measurements. For the batik piece, we used strips that were cut 3" wide and different lengths to make it interesting. Or, you can use one piece of fabric for the top and a different one for the lining, like Jen did.

Cut a piece of batting and a piece of lining fabric 2" wider and 2" longer than the top.

Layer the pieces and quilt the quilt with any pattern you like. Stay-stitch the edges, then wash and dry the quilt, to shrink it and add some texture.

Here's a close-up look at the quilted piece. Now it's ready to measure again, so your cover will be a perfect fit.

OPPOSITE: *Batik laptop cover made by Anita quilted with the digitized pattern Leaf Block 7 from Precision Stitch. Black and turquoise cover made by Jen quilted with Jill's Bubbles from the Statler Siblings collection.*

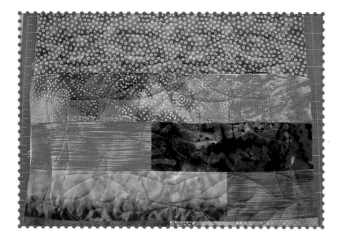

Fold the quilted layers to make a pocket deep enough to hold your laptop. Pin the edges to fit around the sides of the laptop. Make sure it's a comfortable size to slide the laptop in and out. Try it a couple of times before you stitch.

Remove the laptop from the pocket and trim the raw edges 1" from the pinned lines. The extra inch on each side will give you enough fabric to make neat French seams, to cover all the raw edges.

To stitch the envelope with French seams, keep the fabric pocket folded with the right side showing. Stitch a seam ¼" from the raw edges along both sides of the pocket. Trim away any stray threads.

Turn the pocket inside out and stitch the side seams again. This time, make the seams ½" wide, to cover the raw edges of the first seam. A walking foot will help you stitch through all those layers. French seams are the perfect finish because they hide all the raw edges and they won't ravel!

To trim the flap, lay the laptop cover on a table. It should be inside out, with the flap open. Use small scissors to clip into the sides of the flap, just above the seams so the flap can lie flat.

Turn the envelope right-side out. Use a rotary cutter and ruler to trim the edges of the flap on each side. Cut the edges in a straight line to make the flap the same width as the pocket.

Put the laptop inside. Fold the flap down to close the pocket and decide how long you'd like the flap to be. Trim it to that size.

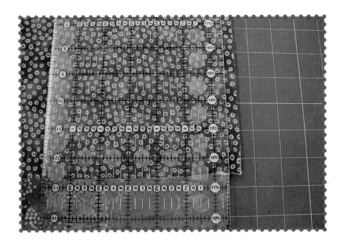

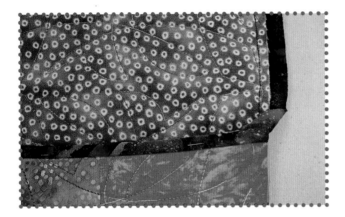

To bind the raw edges, cut bias strips 2" wide and sew pieces together to make a strip long enough to cover all of the raw edges of the top opening and the flap. Fold the strip in half wrong sides together and press with the iron.

Use a ¼" wide seam allowance to stitch the raw edges of the strip to the right side of the quilted cover.

Wrap the binding strip around the raw edge and stitch the folded edge to the lining. We did the final stitching by hand. Be sure the binding covers the line of machine stitching so it doesn't show on the inside.

For more complete information on applying a binding with mitered corners, see page 64.

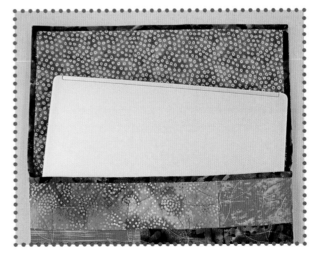

Add a fastener or decorative embellishment, if you like.

This laptop cover made by Anita was quilted with Dragonfly 1 from Precision Stitch.

Easy Sew Poncho

Seamstress Amber

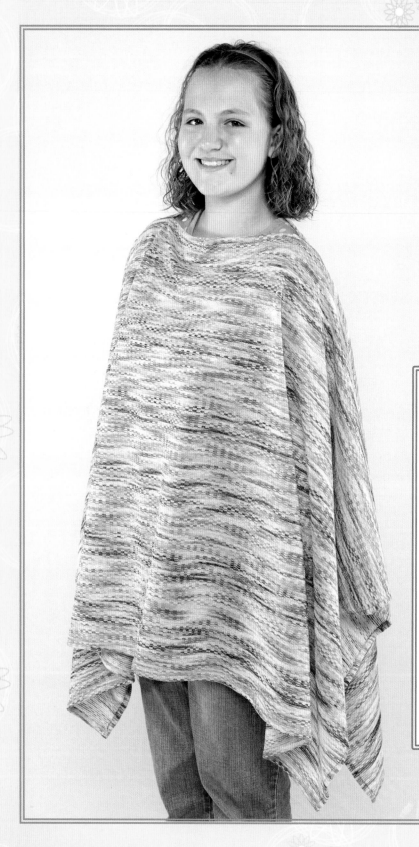

The Big Tools
✓ Sewing machine with a zigzag stitch
✓ Rotary cutter, mat, and ruler
✓ Iron and ironing board

Other Gear
✓ Scissors
✓ Pins
✓ Measuring tape
✓ Masking tape

Supplies
✓ 1½ to 2 yards of fabric
✓ Thread to match

Guest model Makenzie Pegram

Set a fashion trend with a poncho you make yourself. Seersucker would be a good cover-up for the pool; a sweater knit or fleece can keep you warm at a football game; and a dressy fabric will be pretty for a dance. They're so easy, you can make lots of them.

Amber in a poncho she made for herself.

Recommended fabrics for this poncho include wool or rayon challis, seersucker or other cotton fabric, fleece, or sheer fashion fabric. Plaids and stripes can be used for this project, but directional prints like flowering vines might not be good choices, because the pattern will run sideways.

A 45" wide fabric will make a poncho approximately 20" in length (from the neckline down the front and back); a 54" wide fabric will make a poncho approximately 25" in length.

For a personalized fit, have a friend measure your outstretched arms from fingertip to fingertip to decide how much fabric you need. This measurement allows a little extra for shrinkage and for straightening. Amber's measurement was 64" so we bought 2 yards (36" + 36") of fabric.

Beverly and Willow measure Amber.

Easy Sew Poncho

Cut the fabric:

Trim both ends of the fabric to straighten them. Cut the fabric down the middle, length-wise, to make two long narrow rectangles. One piece will be the front of your poncho and one piece will be the back.

Amber uses the rotary cutter to cut the pieces for her poncho.

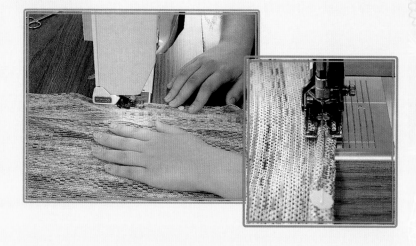

Finish the edges:

Hem each piece of fabric on all four sides. Fold over each edge ¼" twice, to make a narrow hem or use a serger to finish the edges.

Sew the pieces together:

Fold each rectangle of fabric in half crossways to find the center of the top edge. Measure from the middle, 6" each direction, to make a 12" neck opening.

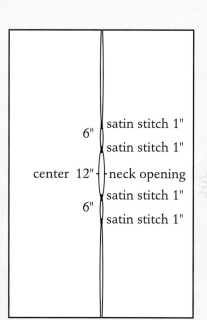

6" — satin stitch 1"
satin stitch 1"
center 12" — neck opening
6" — satin stitch 1"
satin stitch 1"

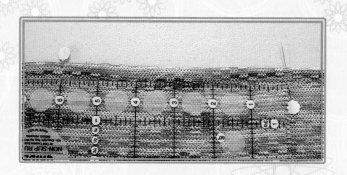

Lay the pieces out flat, with the top edges side by side. Use tape to hold the edges close to each other and to mark a 1" stitching length. Use a zigzag satin stitch to join the edges.

Measure 6" from the end of the stitching and stitch 1" again to create the peek-a-boo shoulder opening.

Note: Smaller children will need smaller measurements. To personalize the fit, the stitched areas should fall in the hollow of the shoulders and in the middle of the upper arms.

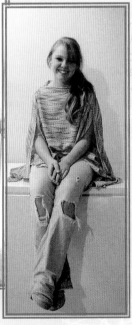

Amber models her new poncho.

Home Dec
Christmas or Holiday Ornaments

The Big Tools
✓ Iron and ironing board

Other Gear
✓ Scissors

✓ Pins

✓ Hand sewing needles

✓ Template material

Supplies
✓ A variety of Christmas or holiday fabrics

✓ Fusible batting

✓ Embroidery floss

✓ Buttons, sequins, charms, puff paint, or other trims

Look at these sweet ornaments. This year I'm gonna decorate the tree with things I made myself.

Christmas or Holiday Ornaments

Decorate the tree or house with ornaments you make yourself. Make extras to share with family and friends!

Don't put the iron directly on the fusible batting.

Prepare the fabrics:

Follow the manufacturer's directions to fuse a piece of fabric to each side of a layer of fusible batting. Using a different fabric on each side makes the ornaments more interesting. Use a non-stick pressing sheet if necessary.

Cut out the shapes:

Trace the shapes from the pattern pages onto card stock or template plastic. Cut them out on the line. Use the templates to trace the shapes onto the layered fabrics and cut them out on the line.

Christmas or Holiday Ornaments

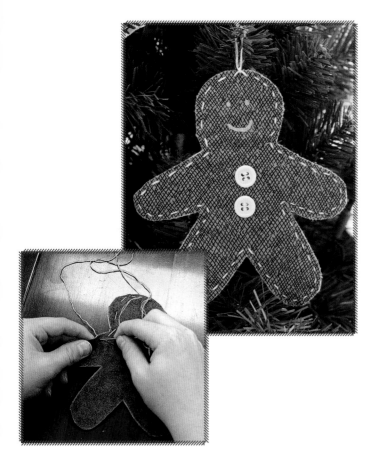

Add some stitching:

Use hand stitching, machine blanket stitch, or other decorative stitches to sew around the edges of your ornaments.

Hint! If you start and stop your hand stitching at the top, you can leave long tails to tie together for a hanger. The thread tails can also be tied in a bow or used to add a button.

Embellish your ornaments:

Sew on buttons, beads, sequins, or other embellishments for even more fun.

Use an assortment of threads, floss, buttons, and other embellishments to decorate your ornaments.

Decorate the tree!
Add a wire hanger and hang your ornaments on the tree.

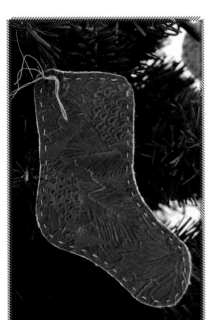

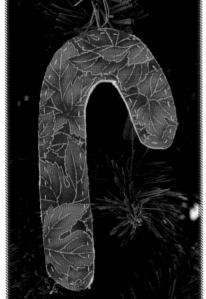

Christmas
or
Holiday Ornaments

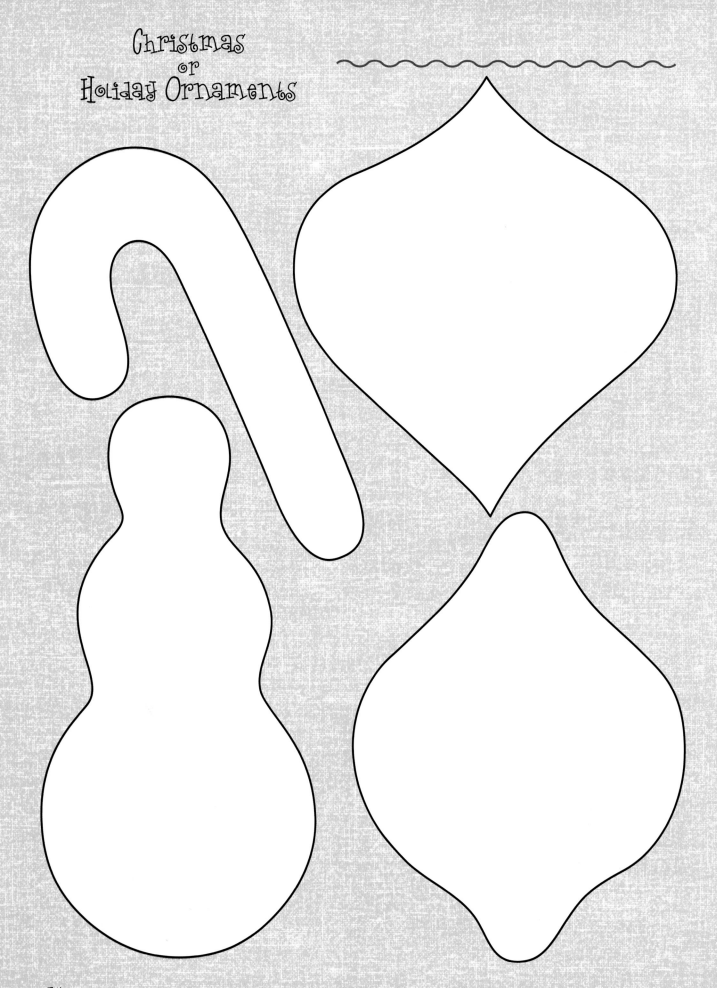

Christmas
or
Holiday Ornaments

BFF Pillow

The BFF pillow is adorable!! Luv U!

The Big Tools
✓ Sewing machine with specialty feet for piecing and quilting
✓ Rotary cutter, mat, and ruler
✓ Iron and ironing board

Other Gear
✓ Scissors
✓ Pins
✓ Hand sewing needles
✓ Masking tape

Supplies
✓ 1 yard of fabric in drapery weight, lightweight denim, or corduroy
✓ 8" square of upholstery vinyl
✓ 20" pillow form or bag of fiberfill for stuffing

Our BFF (Best Friends Forever) Pillow is an uneven nine-patch design with folded pockets in the corners for notes or keep-sakes, and a vinyl window pocket in the middle to display a favorite photo. Sweet!

Amber, Willow, and Seayra

Cut the fabric pieces:

7½" square for the center

Twelve 5" squares for the pocket corners

Four 5" x 7½" rectangles

Two 2½" x 18" framing strips

Two 2½" x 22" framing strips

One 21" square for pillow back

One 21" square of muslin (optional)

One square of batting (optional—if you want to quilt the pillow back)

One square 7" x 7½" of vinyl

WOF (width of fabric)

Pillow back 21" square	5"		Cut twelve 5" squares
7½" square		Cut four 5" x 7½" rectangles	
22" x 2½"	18" x 2½"		
22" x 2½"	18" x 2½"		

selvage

1 yard (36")

Make the pocket squares:

Fold eight squares into triangles right-side out, and press them with the iron.

You will need one square and two folded triangles for each corner pocket.

Lay two triangles on top of each background square. Line up the raw edges at the sides and the bottom corners.

Pin the layers together so they won't slip while you sew. Baste the raw edges together. Use a long stitch length and stitch close to the edges, so the basting stitches won't show later.

Make the window pocket:

Layer the window vinyl over the large center square. Line up the edges on three sides. The uneven edge will be the pocket opening.

Don't put pins through the vinyl! Use tape to hold the uneven (top) edges together. Trim the ends of the tape so they don't get caught in the stitching.

Turn the layered pieces upside down (with vinyl on the bottom) and baste with the machine, to hold the three even edges together. Don't sew across the top edge.

Piece the front of the pillow cover:

Arrange the pieces as shown and piece the nine-patch pillow center. Add framing strips to the top and bottom. Trim the edges even at the corners. Add framing strips to each side and trim them to the correct length. Press your seams as you add each new piece. Be careful not to put the iron on the vinyl window.

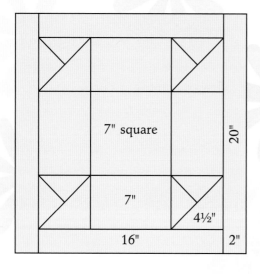

Luv U!

Quilt the back of the pillow cover:

We like to quilt the back of our pillows because it makes them stronger and adds good looking texture. If you want to quilt the back of your pillow, layer it with batting and the block of muslin and quilt a grid or other pattern to hold the layers together.

Finish the pillow cover:

Layer the pillow cover top and back with right sides together, and stitch around the edges. For younger children, we usually say, "put pretty sides together" and stitch. Leave an opening on one side so you can turn the pillow cover right-side out.

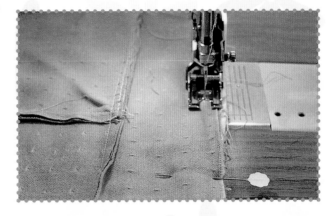

Trim across the corners to remove some bulk from the seam allowance. Turn the pillow cover right-side out and push out the corners. Stuff it as full as you like or insert a pillow form. Sew the opening closed.

Note: We like loose stuffing instead of a pillow form because it fills the corners better. You can make the pillow as soft or as firm as you like, and the finished pillow can be any size.

RIGHT: *Denim BFF pillow with boys' picture – Brandon and Dakota*

Message
or
Photo Board

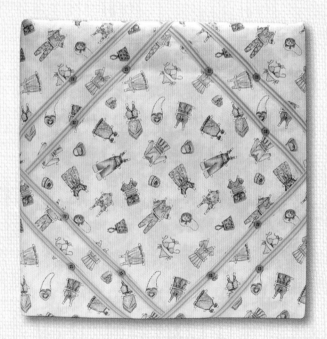

Beastly!!

The Big Tools
- ✓ Rotary cutter, mat, and rulers
- ✓ Iron and ironing board

Other Gear
- ✓ Staple gun – optional
- ✓ Small wood screws 4" x ¾" and a screwdriver
- ✓ Scissors
- ✓ Large straight pins

Supplies
- ✓ Pink foam insulation board
- ✓ Extra lofty poly batting
- ✓ 1 yard fabric
- ✓ 4–6 yards of ribbon or other trim
- ✓ General purpose white glue
- ✓ Decorative buttons

A message board is the perfect place to keep notes, photos, and reminders. Tuck items behind the ribbons or use a pin to hold them tight.

Have an adult cut the insulation board:

If you start with a 4' x 8' foam insulation board and cut down the center to make two pieces, each will be 24" wide. From each of these panels you can cut four 24" x 24" boards.

Cut the batting:

Cut two pieces of batting 24" x 30". Wrap one piece of batting in each direction, as shown in the photo. This will give you two layers of batting on the front for texture, a single layer around the edges and no extra bulk in the corners. Wrap the edges and use glue to hold the batting in place.

Cut the fabric:

Cut a square of fabric 32" x 32". This will give you 4" extra to wrap around on all sides. It's a good idea for the fabric to wrap further than the batting on the back. A single layer of fabric will staple into place more easily if it doesn't have batting underneath it.

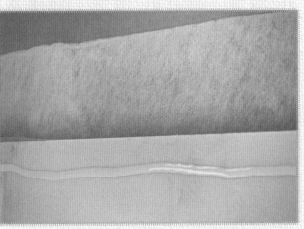

Message or Photo Board

Lay the fabric wrong-side up on a table and lay the covered board on top of it. Wrap the fabric around the edges of the board and use straight pins to temporarily hold it in place. Miter the corners by folding the corner point back, first one side and then the other side.

Turn the board over and check that the fabric looks nice on the front. Smooth out any wrinkles or uneven places.

Finish the edges:

When you are happy with the fabric placement, turn under the raw edges on the back. Use glue to hold everything in place, then pin it again to secure it and let it dry.

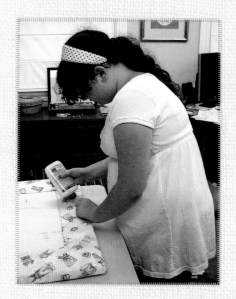

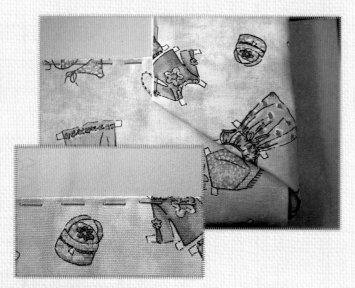

After the glue has dried, check to see if the edges are good and tight. If they are, then it's done. If you think it needs to be more secure, ask an adult to help you use a staple gun to staple the edges, as shown.

Add the ribbons:

Add ribbon, rickrack, sequin tape, shoe laces, or other trim to the front. Decide on the placement of your ribbons. Study the pattern suggestions on page 47 or make up your own.

Cut the ribbons to the right length and pin them into place on the front of the board.

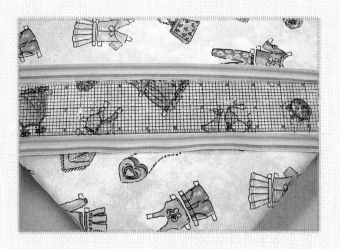

Turn the board over and wrap the ribbon ends to the back. Sometimes you might need an extra hand to control everything. Glue the ends into place on the back of the board and use pins to hold them until they are dry. We used both glue and staples to hold the ends of the ribbon in place on the back of our board.

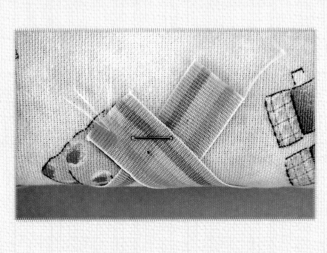

Message or Photo Board

Fasten the ribbons to the front:

Decide where you want buttons to be placed on the front of the board to "quilt" your ribbons and fabrics together.

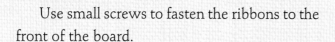

Use small screws to fasten the ribbons to the front of the board.

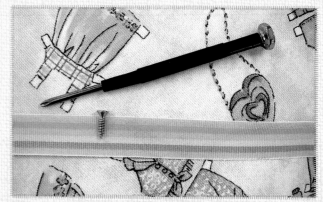

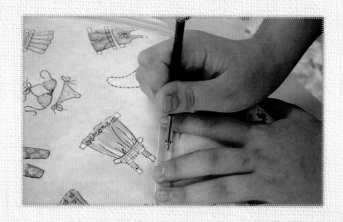

Hold onto the ribbon so it doesn't twist as the screw goes in.

Use a little glue and a button to cover the top of the screw.

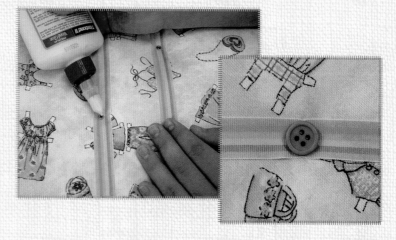

Made by Samantha

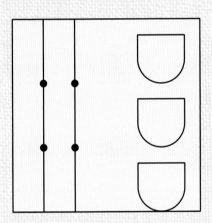

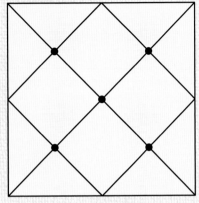

Message board design ideas!

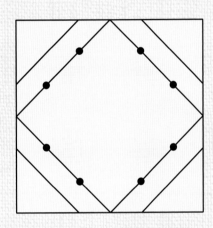

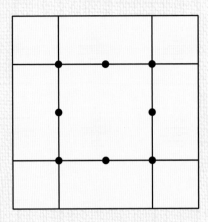

Made by Kaitlin

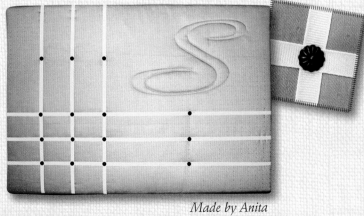

Made by Anita

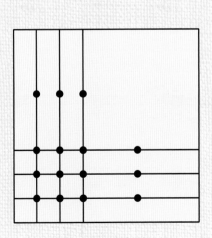

Table Skirt with a Ruched Ruffle

The Big Tools
✓ Sewing machine with specialty feet for quilting
✓ Rotary cutter, mat, and rulers
✓ Iron and ironing board

Other Gear
✓ Scissors
✓ Pins
✓ Hand sewing needles
✓ Measuring tape
✓ RucheMark Strip Ruching Guide
✓ Fabric marking pencil

Supplies
✓ 3½ yards of fabric
✓ A square of batting 4" larger than your table top
✓ A square of muslin 4" larger than your table top
✓ Thread for piecing and quilting

Hey! I luv ur table skirt n ur room! U should totally make me 1. Thx! Luv u lotz.

Amber works on her table skirt.

If you like to sew, this table skirt is a sweet project.

The top is quilted and the skirt is ruched—gathered in a special pattern to make petals around the top.

Note: Most table skirts can be made from 3½ yards of fabric. If your table is large, look at this worksheet to find out how much you will need.

Cut your fabric:

Cut a square of fabric that is 4" larger than the top of your table. Then cut the rest of the fabric into three long panels to make the ruffled skirt.

Sew the skirt:

Sew the panels of the table skirt together side by side to form a tube. Press the seams open.

Worksheet:

Calculating Yardage for the Table Skirt

1. Measure around the top of the table to find the perimeter. _____"

2. Multiply the perimeter by 2 to find total inches of fabric needed for gathering the table skirt. _____"

3. Divide the total inches by the width of the fabric to determine how many panels you will need for your table skirt. _____panels.

4. Measure the height of the table and add 6" to determine the length of one panel. _____"

5. Multiply the length of fabric from #4 by the number of panels needed. _____"

6. Measure across the top of the table and add 4". _____"
Add this to the measurement in #5. _____"

7. Divide the total inches by 36 to determine how many yards of fabric to buy.

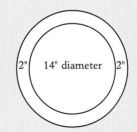

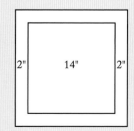

Table top and seam allowance examples

Table Skirt with a Ruched Ruffle

Make the quilted top:

Layer the square of fabric with squares of batting and muslin the same size and quilt a pretty pattern. This pattern is Flower Power designed by Mary Eddy.

Trace the top of the table onto paper to make a template. Lay the paper template on the back (muslin side) of the quilted piece and trace around it. Trim the quilted piece ½" larger all around to create a seam allowance.

Finish the cut edges with a zigzag stitch.

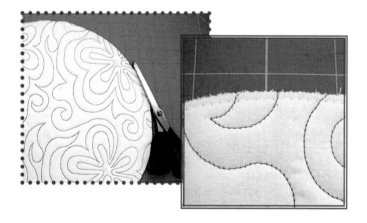

Ruche the skirt:

Fold a 1" hem in the top edge of the skirt fabric and press.

Use a pencil or fabric marker and draw the extra-large strip ruching pattern from the RucheMark Strip Ruching Guide on the hem. The pointed ends of the pattern go toward the folded edge.

For ruching by machine, use a large basting stitch and a STRONG thread and follow the marked lines. Pull the bobbin thread (the one on the right side of the fabric) and gather the skirt to fit around the table top. Tie the thread tails together to make a strong knot.

OR, for ruching by hand, use a matching quilting thread to gather the marked fabric, following the ruching pattern. Gather until the ruched edge fits around the table top.

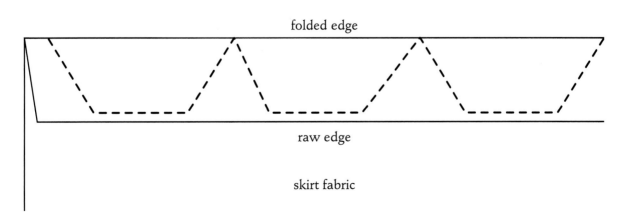

folded edge

raw edge

skirt fabric

Extra large ruching pattern

Table Skirt with a Ruched Ruffle

Attach the ruched skirt to the quilted top:

Pin the ruffled skirt into place around the edges of the quilted top. Both pieces (top and skirt) should be right-side up and the ruched edge should overlap the raw edges of the top. Adjust the gathers so they are even all around.

Using a zigzag stitch and following the line of gathering stitches, sew the skirt to the quilted top. A walking foot on the machine will help stitch this line without pushing the ruffles out of place.

Hem the bottom edge:

Turn up ¼" at the bottom of the table skirt and stitch all around. This will create a finished edge on your hem.

Put the skirt on the table and measure the finished length. Would you like the skirt to just touch the floor or would you like it longer and puddled? Pin up the hem to the length you like and then use the machine to stitch the hem in place.

Collage Wall Quilts

18" X 20"

The Big Tools
- ✓ Sewing machine with zigzag or decorative stitches and specialty feet for appliqué and quilting
- ✓ Rotary cutter with straight and wavy blades
- ✓ Cutting mat and ruler
- ✓ Iron and ironing board

Other Gear
- ✓ Scissors
- ✓ Pins
- ✓ Hand sewing needles
- ✓ Digital camera

Supplies
- ✓ One fat quarter of background fabric
- ✓ One fat quarter of muslin or fabric for quilt back
- ✓ Standard ⅛ yard of fabric for binding
- ✓ Fusible web
- ✓ Batting 20" x 22"
- ✓ Variety of thread colors
- ✓ A favorite t-shirt you are not wearing any more
- ✓ Embellishments

Dragon Swirls, made by Amber Perdue
Amber loved this T shirt with a curly, swirly dragon. For embellishments, she added beads, shells, an origami flower, a peace sign, and playing cards she altered to spell the word Love. Her background quilting pattern is Lilies in the Water by Ellen Munnich.

OMG! YOUR QUILT IS FAB!

Collage Wall Quilts

See how a favorite T-shirt, theme quilting, and cool embellishments can come together to make a personalized wall quilt.

Start by collecting a few things that will say something about who you are, what you like to do, or remind you of special times. Good ideas would be:

badges from sports, scouts, or other activities

4-H ribbons

wrist band/sweat band

beads or buttons

coins

sea shells

shoestrings/hair ties

yarn/rickrack

jewelry

music discs

neck tie

handkerchief

silk flowers

movie or sports tickets

prom souvenirs

real photos or photo transfers

EARTH SERVICE, *made by Willow Buckelew*

Willow chose a green theme for her collage quilt. Her T shirt is from the Earth Service Corps at the YMCA. She added embellishments to reflect nature and her wish for peace. Willow's background quilting pattern is Autumn in Oregon designed by Janice Bahrt.

RIGHT: *SK8, made by Brandon Perdue*

Brandon decided on a sports theme for his collage quilt. The embellishments he chose show his interests in fishing, golfing, skateboarding, and music. Brandon quilted his background with a pattern called Broken Glass by Deb Kerr.

Prepare your fabrics:

You can wash and dry your fabrics or use them as they are. Press the wrinkles out of all the fabrics before you start to work with them.

Quilt your quilt:

Layer the top fabric, the batting, and the back. Think about whether your quilt will look better with the longer measurement up and down or sideways. Quilt the quilt now, to add a background pattern and to hold the layers together. Use a sewing machine with a walking foot, quilt with free-motion if you know how, or use a longarm machine if you have access to one. Choose a quilting pattern that will fit the mood of your quilt. These young quilters chose a variety of patterns to go with music, sports, and nature.

ABOVE: *Brandon had a good time testing programmed stitches on the sewing machine.*

LEFT: *Amber quilts a design with the longarm machine.*

Add the t-shirt:

Cut the decorative part from your t-shirt and place it where you think it looks best on your quilt. Pin the edges to hold the t-shirt fabric in place.

Stitch along the edges of the t-shirt, using a straight stitch, zigzag stitch, or other decorative stitch. A walking foot will be helpful to keep the t-shirt fabric from scooting around. Trim away the extra fabric close to your stitching line.

Collage Wall Quilts

Bind your quilt:

Decide on the final size for your wall quilt. Use a rotary cutter and mat to trim the edges. You will bind the quilt now, before the embellishments are added.

For a funky edge, you can make a wavy, fusible binding. Here's how!

Follow the manufacturer's directions to add fusible web to the wrong side of your binding fabric. Use a rotary cutter with a wavy blade to cut strips 2" wide and long enough for each edge of your quilt.

WITH THE FUSIBLE WEB PAPER STILL IN-SIDE, fold the strips in half and press to make a crease in the binding. Pull out the paper and tuck the edge of the quilt into the folded binding strip. Use the iron to fuse the binding into place on both the front and the back. Trim extra fabric from the ends. Do all four sides the same way. Use the sewing machine and the walking foot to topstitch the binding into place.

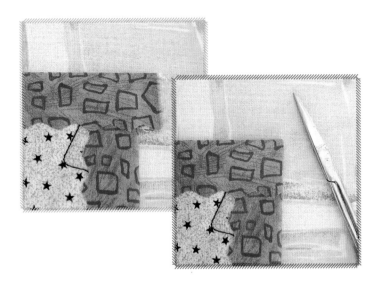

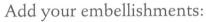

Brandon and Amber work on binding.

Add your embellishments:

Audition your embellishments. Move them around until you are happy with the way the quilt looks. Take digital photos as you work. When you decide on the final arrangement, save the photo for reference.

Pictures can be stitched across the corners or stitched through all around the edges. Jewelry can be stitched on by hand or may be pinned on. Dimensional items, like a golf tee, sea shell, coin, or other souvenir might be hand stitched on or they can be held in place under a layer of netting or clear plastic.

If you took a picture, use it to help you remember how you wanted things arranged, but feel free to change your mind if a better idea comes along!

Impressions
22" X 22"

RUBBER AND STEEL, *made by Blake*

PATTERNS, *made by Seayra*

The Big Tools
✓ Sewing Machine with specialty feet for piecing and quilting
✓ Rotary cutter, mat, and ruler
✓ Iron and ironing board

Other Gear
✓ Scissors
✓ Pins
✓ Hand sewing needles
✓ Masking tape
✓ Digital camera

Supplies
✓ Sheets of plain paper
✓ Brown paper grocery bag
✓ Several crayons in colors you like
✓ Pen for taking notes
✓ Fat quarter of fabric to color
✓ 1⅛ yards of fabric for borders, back, and binding
✓ Paint sticks (optional)
✓ Batting
✓ Sewing thread and transparent quilting thread

re you ready for an outdoor adventure? Pack up paper, pencil, and the other non-quilting supplies and get ready to record your "impressions." Take a walk in the park or along your street, looking for things that have interesting textures.

An impression of a raised or incised pattern, taken by covering it with a piece of paper and rubbing across it with a drawing tool, is called a "rubbing."

First, use paper and crayon to make test rubbings on different surfaces such as stone, tree bark, or leaves. You might want to keep a journal of the textures you liked best and where you found them.

Journal page created by Beverly

BRANDON'S PARK IMPRESSIONS, *made by Brandon*

SHADES OF AMBER, *made by Amber*

Impressions

Repeat your favorite rubbings using fabric and crayons or paint sticks to make blocks for your IMPRESSIONS quilt.

ABOVE: *Brandon found good texture on an old metal plate.*

LEFT: *Seayra picks up an impression from tree bark.*

Cut your blocks bigger than you need and use masking tape to hold the edges in place while you color. We started with 10" blocks and trimmed them to 8½" when they were finished.

ABOVE: *Amber liked the woodgrain pattern in the picnic shelter.*

RIGHT: *This old tree stump made a good block for Brandon's quilt.*

Blake decided to start his quilt blocks in his grandpa's motorcycle shop. He found great textures everywhere and his big crayons did a good job of picking up the impressions.

ABOVE: *Dave, Blake, and Elisa take a rubbing from a vintage motorcycle tire.*

LEFT: *Elisa helps Blake pick up a steel impression.*

Teens & Tweens ✄ Anita Shackelford & Jennifer Perdue

To make an indoor rubbing:

Some items, like this sunflower leaf from the garden, can be brought inside. Lay it on a smooth table top or a layer of plastic.

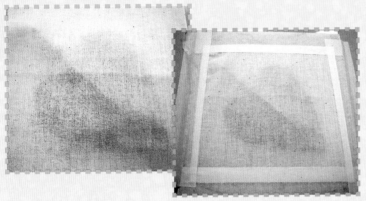

Lay the square of fabric on top, right-side up.

Use masking tape to hold all of the edges of the fabric, so it doesn't wiggle while you do the coloring.

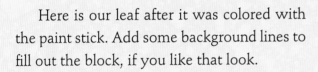

Here is our leaf after it was colored with the paint stick. Add some background lines to fill out the block, if you like that look.

If you used paint to create the impression, follow the manufacturer's directions and let it dry.

Then use an iron to heat set the paint or crayon and make it permanent. Place the block colored-side down on a sheet of heavy brown paper or a grocery bag. Press with the hottest setting for 10–15 seconds. Some of the color will transfer to the paper, so don't move the block around while you iron. The finished block will be hot, so be careful when you pick it up.

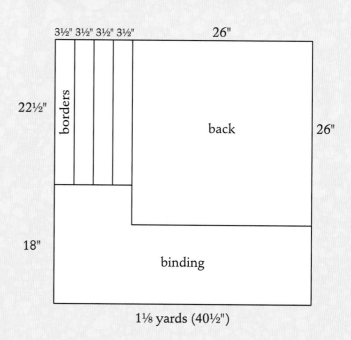

Piece the quilt top:

Trim the blocks to remove any frayed edges and make them all the same size.

Lay out your blocks on the table and decide how you want them to be arranged.

We put four blocks together to make the center of our quilt. Use the sewing machine and a ¼" seam to sew two blocks together for the top row and two blocks together for the bottom row. Then sew the rows together.

Add a border:

We used hand-dyed fabric for some of our quilts. Or, choose a print that looks good with your rubbings, like Blake did in his motorcycle quilt.

Cut strips of fabric 3½" wide and as long as you need for your quilt top. Sew borders to the top and bottom and press them to the outside. Trim the corners, if you need to, to make them square. Add the side borders in the same way.

3½" 3½" 3½" 3½"   26"

22½"   borders   back   26"

18"   binding

1⅛ yards (40½")

Quilt your quilt:

We discovered that contrasting threads and fancy quilting patterns competed with our colored designs. Transparent or matching thread and simple quilting will be the best way to finish your quilt. The quilting pattern we chose for the blocks is Grid and Frame, designed by Tanya del Tongo Armanasco and Anita.

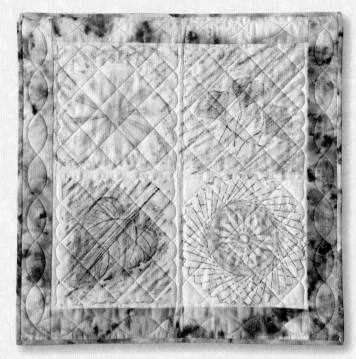

CUT GLASS AND GARDEN LEAVES, made by Anita

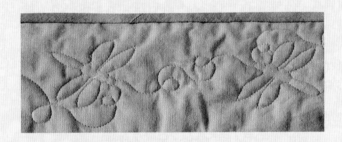

Border quilting pattern ideas:

Amber quilted her border with Double Dragonfly, designed by Marty Vint.

Brandon quilted his border with an African Leaf pattern, designed by Anita.

Seayra chose a Heart Leaf pattern for her borders, designed by Anita.

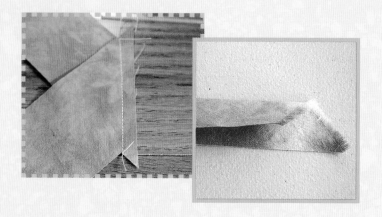

Double Bias Binding

Cut bias strips 2" wide and sew them together with a bias seam. Make enough binding to fit around the edges of your quilt.

Fold the strip in half right-side out, and press with the iron.

Line up the raw edges of the binding with the raw edges of the quilt and sew with a ¼" seam. Start sewing in the middle of the top edge of the quilt. Leave a few inches of the binding unsewn at the beginning. You will sew that beginning tail to the end of the binding when you get all the way around.

A walking foot will help keep the layers from shifting as you sew. Adjust the needle or the foot to be sure you are sewing a ¼" seam.

Sew along the first edge. Be sure to keep your seam an even distance from the edge of the quilt. Stop sewing ¼" away from the corner.

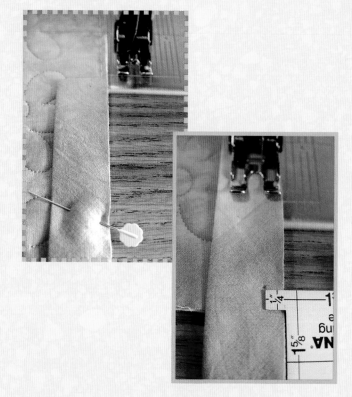

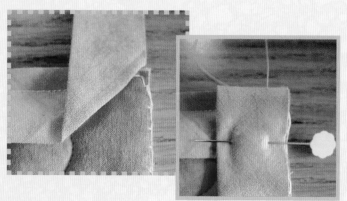

Fold the binding strip up to form a miter.

Fold the strip down to begin sewing the next side. The folded edge at the top of the binding should line up with the raw edge of the quilt.

Sew a ¼" seam along the second side. Be sure to stop ¼" from the next corner and fold another miter.

When you have sewn almost all the way around, lay the unsewn binding strip on top of the tail at the beginning of the binding.

Measure a seam allowance so you can sew the ends together with a smooth bias seam. The amount of seam allowance should be 2", the same as the width of the binding strip. Cut straight across the end of the binding on this line.

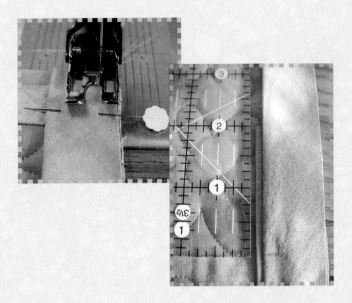

Overlap the beginning and end of the binding strips with right sides together, to make a bias seam. Draw a line from the corner of the underneath strip to the corner of the strip on top. Sew on this diagonal line, as shown, and trim away the extra fabric.

Press the seam open. Fold the strip again. Line up the raw edges and finish sewing the binding to the quilt.

Daisy Frame border quilting pattern designed by Marty Vint; adapted from the Precision Stitch pattern Daisy 4

Wrap the folded edge of the binding around the raw edges and sew it to the back of the quilt. You can use straight pins to hold the binding in place while you sew. We liked using hair clips because they hold on tight and don't poke us while we work.

When you stitch your binding, be sure to use a matching color of thread and take small stitches that don't show. The binding should cover the line of stitching made by the sewing machine.

LEFT: *Amber and Seayra have some fun while they work on their bindings.*

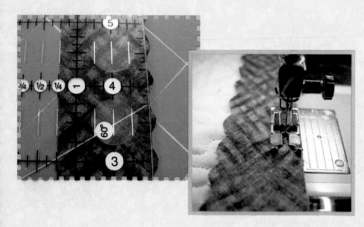

Here's a quick way to bind your quilt with the sewing machine!

Rippled Raw Edge Binding

Cut bias strips with a straight cut on one side. Use a fancy rotary-cutter blade to cut the other side. The width of the strip should be 1¼" plus the extra rippled edge.

Line up the raw edge of the quilt and the raw edge of the binding. You will be sewing the right side of the binding to the back of the quilt. When you put it under the sewing machine, both pieces should be wrong-side up. Sew the single layer binding to the back of the quilt with a ¼" seam. Miter the corners, as shown in the binding instructions on page 64.

Wrap the rippled edge of the binding around to the front of the quilt. Put pins in from the back to hold the binding in place. Fold a miter at each corner on the front.

Use a walking foot to sew in the ditch from the back of the quilt. Your line of stitches should catch the binding on the front and the raw edges will show.

The wavy edge makes a cool frame for your wall quilt. If you put this kind of binding on a bed quilt, the bias edges will get soft and fuzzy when you wash it.

BELOW: *RUBBER AND STEEL, made by Blake*

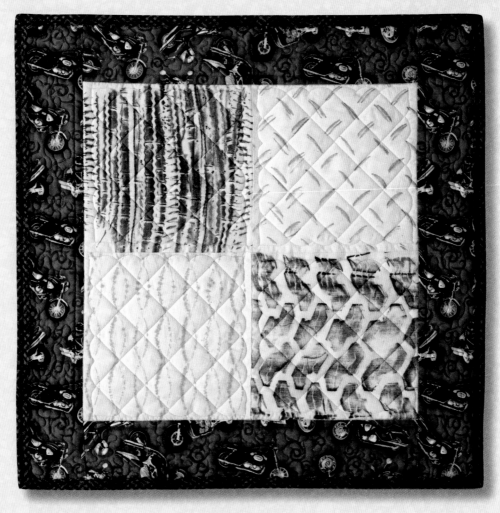

Paint Ball Party
57" X 57"

The Big Tools
- ✓ Sewing machine with specialty feet for piecing, appliqué and quilting
- ✓ Rotary cutter, mat, and rulers
- ✓ Iron and ironing board

Other Gear
- ✓ Scissors
- ✓ Pins
- ✓ Hand sewing needles
- ✓ Digital camera
- ✓ Non-stick pressing sheet

Supplies
- ✓ 6 yards of fabric for borders, back, and binding
- ✓ 2–2½ yards of solids and graphic prints in saturated paint box colors
- ✓ Fusible web for appliqué
- ✓ Batting 60" x 60"
- ✓ Thread in a variety of colors

The PAINT BALL PARTY quilt is easy to make because every block is the same. It's the twist-and-turn placement that makes the balls bounce!

Cut 81 4½" squares for background blocks. We used solid colors for backgrounds.

Cut strips 1½" wide for the framing strips. Half of your strips will be cut 4½" long and half will be 5½" long. Cut a stack of each length to start. You will need 81 of each length, but it's a good idea to audition color combinations as you go. We used solids and a few batiks for the strips.

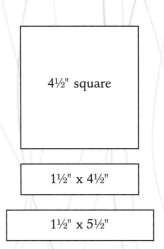

4½" square

1½" x 4½"

1½" x 5½"

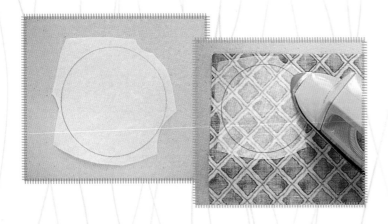

Prepare the circles:

Follow these step-by-step directions for fusible appliqué and make 81 circles:

Draw the circle on the paper side of the fusible web. Cut out the circle with some extra paper all around. Follow the manufacturer's directions to apply the fusible to the wrong side of each fabric.

Cut out the circle on the drawn line. Peel off the paper backing.

OPPOSITE: *PAINT BALL PARTY is quilted with a digitized pattern called Fireworks, designed by Kim Diamond.*

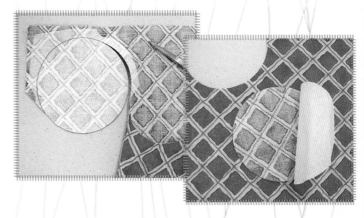

Now the fun begins!

You'll need one background square, one circle, one short strip, and one long strip for each block. Play with the pieces. Mix and match to make combinations you think look good together.

Take your time and enjoy the colors. Rearrange some of the sets if you change your mind. Cut more pieces if you don't have what you need.

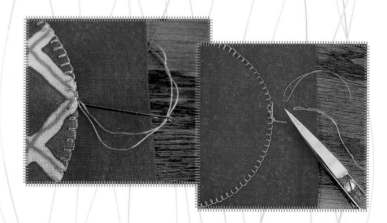

Appliqué the circles:

Use the iron and a pressing sheet to attach the circle to the center of the background square.

Appliqué the circle to the background with a zigzag or a blanket stitch. If your sewing machine has an open-toe or clear appliqué foot, it will help you see the edge of the circle. Turn the block as you go and try to keep your stitches right on the edge.

Start and stop stitching at the same place. Your stitching line will look neater if you pull the thread tails to the back of the block, tie them in a knot, and trim the tails.

Piece the blocks:

Take one appliquéd block and the two framing strips to the sewing machine. Sew the short strip to one side of the block. Fold the strip open and press the seam.

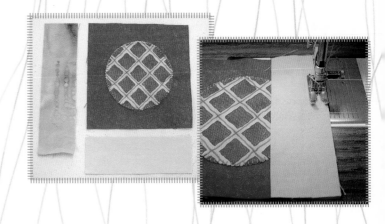

Turn the block and sew a long strip to the next side. Make sure the long strip overlaps the end of the first strip. Fold the strip open and press the seam.

Now you have one finished block!

Keep on sewing until you have made all of the blocks you need. If you line them up all the same, they will look like this (photo 1). But when you twist and turn them, they will begin to bounce around! (photo2)

Arrange your blocks to make the quilt top:

Lay out nine rows of nine bocks across to make the center of your quilt. Twist and turn and rearrange so you don't have the same colors side by side. Study your layout to make sure you are happy with the arrangement. Take digital photos if you can. The pictures will help you remember where everything goes when you start to sew the quilt top together.

Sew the quilt top:

Sew nine blocks together to make each row. Press the seams in the first row to the right; press the seams in the second row to the left. Keep alternating the directions of the seams in each row as you work your way to the bottom. Alternating seams will make it easier to sew the rows together.

When you sew the long row seams, be careful to match the seam lines of the blocks from row to row. Pin to keep them lined up.

Look at the cutting chart to cut four borders and the pieces for the back of your quilt. Add 6½" border strips to the top and bottom of the quilt. Trim the corners to straighten them if you need to. Then add borders to the sides.

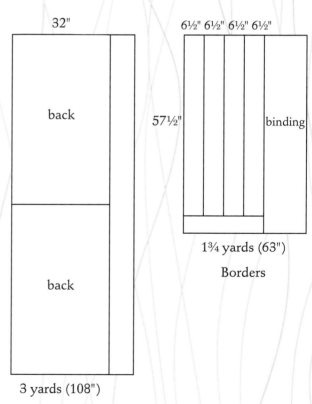

Borders and back cutting chart

Quilt your quilt:

We quilted a wild pattern of swirls and explosions all over this quilt to add to the mood of a paint ball party. Quilt yours any way you like, add a binding, and enjoy your masterpiece!

WALL QUILT PATTERN

Finished sizes:
- 4" square
- 3" circle
- 1" strips

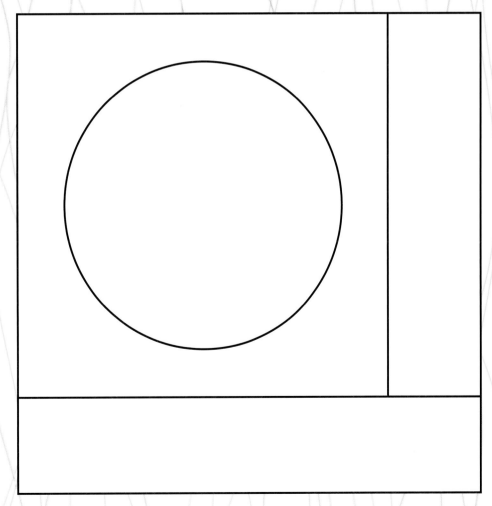

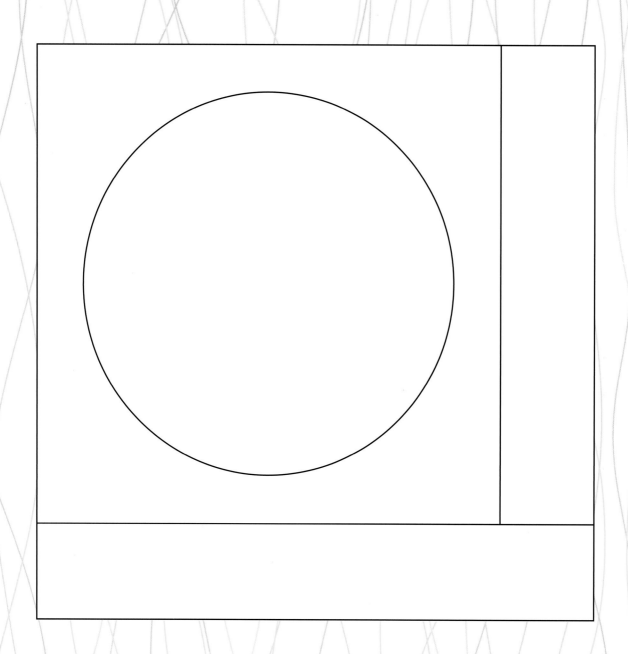

BED QUILT
PATTERN
enlarge 200%

Finished sizes:
  10" square
  8" circle
  2" strips

Amber's Flowers in the Window
84" X 96"

The Big Tools
✓ Sewing machine with ¼" foot and zipper foot
✓ Rotary cutter, mat, and rulers
✓ Iron and ironing board

Other Gear
✓ Scissors
✓ Pins
✓ Hand sewing needles
✓ Digital camera

Supplies
✓ Large print 2 yards
✓ Vine 2 yards
✓ Dot 2 yards
✓ Wavy stripe 2 yards
✓ Solid green 1¼ yards
✓ Brown 3 yards
✓ Back 6 yards
✓ Binding 1 yard
✓ Freezer paper
✓ White glue
✓ Queen size batting

Quilting patterns:
Amber used Window Pane and Curly Sash by Anita, Circle Frame by Jen, Cherry Blossom by Todd Brown, and Ying-Yang Border by Kay Oft.

Amber chose the hip City Girl fabrics from Benartex and made a quilt large enough for her bed. She also decided to piece her circles instead of appliquéing them. If you want more detailed instruction on this piecing method, refer to *Piece-lique: Curves the New Way* by Sharon Schamber. Or, you can follow the directions for PAINT BALL PARTY to appliqué your circles to the background blocks.

The quilt is made of forty-two 12" blocks.

Cut your fabrics:

✖ 42 – 10½" squares from a variety of fabrics to make the "windows"

✖ 42 – 10" circles or squares of fabric from the flower prints that will show through the windows

✖ 42 – 2½" x 10½" strips and

✖ 42 – 2½" x 12½" strips

It's probably a good idea to cut a few pieces or strips at a time and make your color and fabric decisions as you go.

✖ Cut border strips 6½" wide and as long as you need for your quilt.

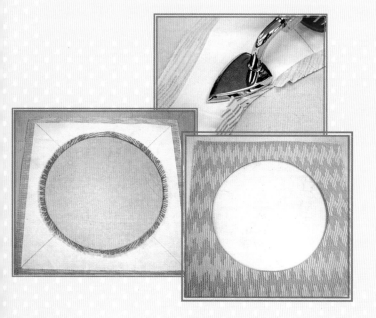

Make your blocks:

Cut a square of freezer paper as large as your background block. Cut the circle shape out of the center. Iron the freezer paper to the wrong side of the fabric. Cut away the center of the fabric to open the window. Be sure to leave a seam allowance that you can clip and iron over the edge of the paper.

Add some drops of white glue to the seam allowance and place your window over the printed fabric. The glue will hold the two layers of fabric together.

RIGHT: *Amber and Jen "Role reversal! I got to show Mom how to do this step."*

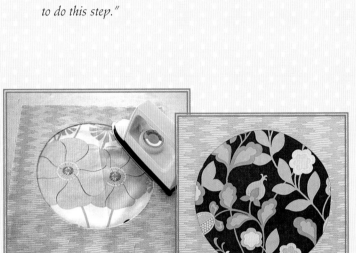

Use the iron to dry the glue and make a sharp line to follow when you sew.

You get to decide what will show through the opening. Amber made a lot of different combinations with her fabrics.

Take your blocks to the sewing machine. Lay the block right-side up and lift up the window layer. Look for the seam allowance line and use a zipper foot to carefully stitch the two layers together.

Trim away any extra fabric after the stitching is finished.

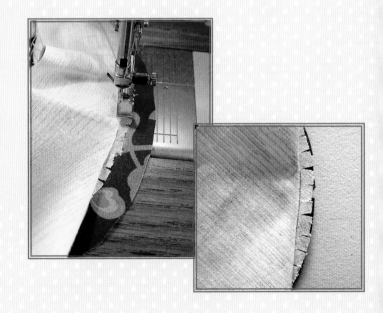

Amber's Flowers in the Window

Because these flower fabrics are directional, Amber couldn't twist and turn her blocks, or she'd have sideways or upside-down flowers! She did her layout on the design wall, finding just the right placement of each color and each print. Then she added her sashing strips between the blocks. We decided to take pictures as she worked on her arrangement. A final picture can help make sure you sew everything together in the right place!

LEFT: *Amber plans the layout of her quilt on the design wall.*

When you have matched up your blocks and strips, take them to the sewing machine and sew them together.

Follow the directions on page 72 for PAINT BALL PARTY for assembling the quilt top and adding the borders.

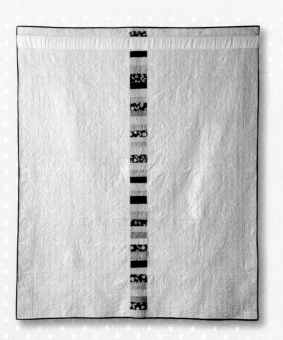

Six yards of fabric cut into two panels and sewn together side-by-side will make a quilt back about 80" wide. Since Amber's quilt was just a little wider than that, she needed something more. Instead of buying another 3 yards of fabric for a third panel, we decided to be creative. Amber used her leftover fabric to make a long, colorful strip and added it in between the two large panels of lining fabric. The extra piece made her backing wide enough and we think it's a cute touch.

Joyful Hearts
48" X 48"

The Big Tools
✓ Sewing machine with specialty feet for piecing, appliqué, and quilting
✓ Rotary cutter, mat, and rulers
✓ Iron and ironing board

Other Gear
✓ Scissors
✓ Pins
✓ Hand sewing needles
✓ Non-stick pressing sheet

Supplies
✓ 4½ yards fabric for background blocks, borders, back, and binding
✓ 1½ yards total of bright prints—we used 15 fabrics
✓ Crib size batting 54" x 60"
✓ Variegrated quilting thread
✓ Buttons

Joyful Hearts

This fun, fresh quilt is made with machine appliqué and button embellishment. Bright colors and "confetti" quilting make it "Joyful."

Cut your blocks and borders:

Look at the cutting chart and cut nine blocks and four borders in the sizes shown.

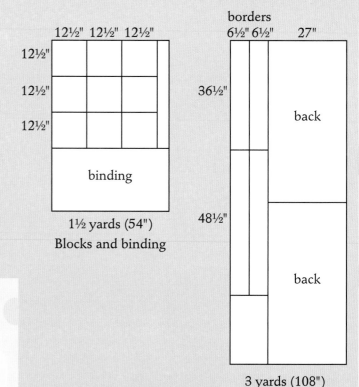

Blocks and binding — 1½ yards (54")

12½" · 12½" · 12½" (top), 12½" · 12½" · 12½" (left side)

binding

borders — 6½" 6½" 27"

36½", 48½"

back

back

3 yards (108")

Borders and back

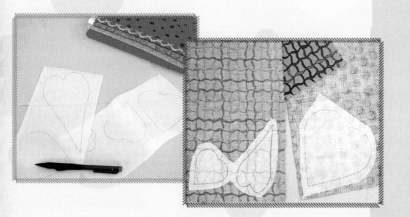

Prepare the fusible appliqué:

Draw the hearts on the paper side of the fusible web.

Choose fabrics for each of the shapes. Follow the manufacturer's directions to apply the fusible to the wrong side of each fabric.

Cut out the hearts, cutting on the drawn line. Peel off the paper backing.

PREVIOUS PAGE: *JOYFUL HEARTS is quilted with a Star and Feather border designed by Anita. Individual stars were added to fill background spaces and a programmed stitch from Bernina added a "confetti" touch.*

Design your blocks:

Arrange the appliqué shapes to fill each block. Be sure to leave room around the edges of the block for seam allowances to sew the blocks together. Also remember to leave space in the background for buttons and quilting designs.

When you are happy with the arrangement, use an iron and a pressing sheet to fuse the hearts into place.

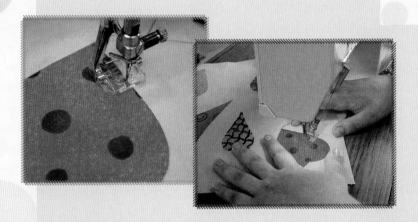

Appliqué the hearts:

Use a blanket stitch, by hand or by machine, to stitch around the edges of the appliqué. A clear or open toe appliqué foot will make it easier to see what you are stitching. Change thread colors, if you like, to coordinate with the colors in each fabric.

Piece the top:

Sew three blocks together to make each row. Press the seams in opposite directions in each row. Sew the rows together to make the center of your quilt. Add borders to the top and bottom and trim to make sure the corners are square. Add the side borders.

Quilt your quilt:

Layer and quilt the quilt with patterns to fill the open spaces. First, we quilted around the edges of the appliqué shapes to stablilize the quilt and make the hearts stand up. Then we quilted stars and confetti curls in between the hearts. The star and feather quilting pattern repeats the star design in the border.

Add some fun:

Add buttons or other embellishments to fill some of the background spaces.

Bind the quilt:

Follow the directions on page 64 for Double Bias Binding, or use one of the other binding techniques to finish your quilt.

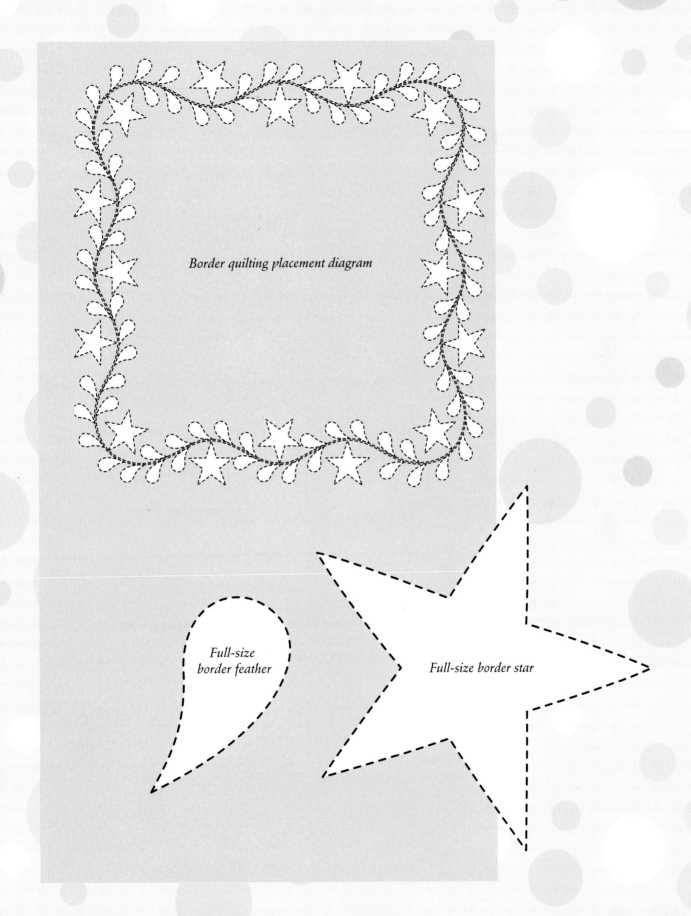

Border quilting placement diagram

Full-size border feather

Full-size border star

Super Star
48" X 48"

The Big Tools
✓ Sewing machine with specialty feet for piecing, appliqué, and quilting
✓ Rotary cutter, mat, and rulers
✓ Iron and ironing board

Other Gear
✓ Scissors
✓ Pins
✓ Hand sewing needles
✓ Non-stick pressing sheet

Supplies
✓ 1½ yards fabric for background blocks and binding
✓ 3 yards fabric for borders and back
✓ 1 yard silver/gray for stars
✓ Fusible web for appliqué
✓ Thread for piecing
✓ Batting
✓ Variegated quilting thread

Teens & Tweens ✂ Anita Shackelford & Jennifer Perdue

Brandon made his appliqué quilt with stars instead of hearts. He used solid colors for the stars and the blocks, and a print fabric for the borders and the back. Think about what makes you a "super star" and follow that theme. Brandon loves to play the drums, so he quilted musical notes into his quilt.

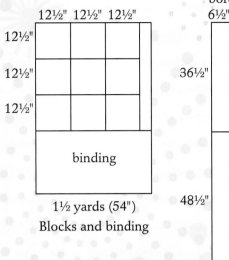

1½ yards (54")
Blocks and binding

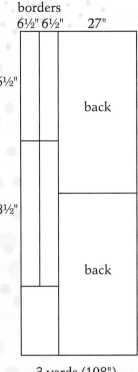

3 yards (108")
Borders and back

Cut your blocks and borders:

Refer to the cutting chart to cut the blocks and borders for the SUPER STAR quilt. The construction steps will be the same as for JOYFUL HEARTS, pages 80–81.

Because all of the stars are cut from the same fabric, it will be easier to iron a large piece of fusible web to the back of the appliqué fabric. Trace the stars and cut them out on the line. Arrange the stars on your background blocks any way you like. Use the iron and a pressing sheet to fuse them into place.

Brandon appliquéd his stars with a straight stitch, following the lines you would use if you were drawing the star with a pencil. The stitching lines through the center of the star make the appliqué stronger.

Brandon uses the longarm machine.

Piece the quilt top:

Sew three blocks together to make each row. Sew the rows together to make the center of the quilt.

Add the borders:

Add borders to the top and bottom. Trim the corners to straighten them if you need to. Add the side borders.

Quilt your quilt:

Choose a quilting pattern that fits your idea of a "Super Star." Brandon decided on a music theme and quilted his quilt with the longarm machine.

LEFT: *The background quilting pattern in SUPER STAR is Music's in the Air designed by Kim Diamond.*

Teens & Tweens ✄ Anita Shackelford & Jennifer Perdue

Mosaic Appliqué
30" X 30"

*Mosaic: A surface decoration made by laying
small pieces of variously colored material to form
a picture or pattern, usually in stone*

The Big Tools
✓ Sewing machine with specialty feet for piecing, appliqué, and quilting
✓ Rotary cutter, mat, and ruler
✓ Iron and ironing board

Other Gear
✓ Scissors
✓ Pins
✓ Hand sewing needles
✓ Non-stick pressing sheet

Supplies
✓ ⅓ yard fabric for background
✓ ½ yard total fabric for appliqué
✓ ⅔ yard fabric for sashing and binding
✓ 1 yard fabric for borders
✓ 1 yard fabric for back and sleeve
✓ 36" x 36" square of batting
✓ Threads in a variety of colors for appliqué
✓ Quilting thread in a color to match background fabric
✓ Floss for hand blanket stitch
✓ Freezer paper or plastic for templates
✓ Fusible web for appliqué

ABOVE: *The kids' Mosaic, made by Willow, Beverly, Amber, Brandon, Jen, and Anita*

Mosaic Appliqué

We made our mosaic out of fabric, of course! Choose a theme, a novelty print, or just work with colors you like— the scrappier the better!

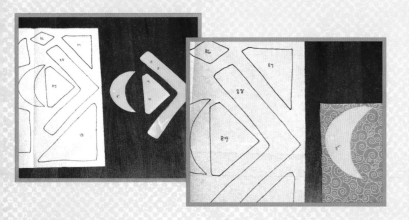

Cut your fabrics:

Cut four background squares 10" x 10".

Trace the appliqué shapes onto freezer paper or template plastic and cut them out.

Study the layout for your blocks and decide which fabrics to put in each place.

Follow the directions for fusible appliqué on page 80 to cut and prepare each piece.

Arrange your appliqué shapes:

Have fun fitting the puzzle pieces together. Be sure to leave a ½" margin at the outside edges of the block, so your appliqué pieces don't look crowded when you sew the blocks together.

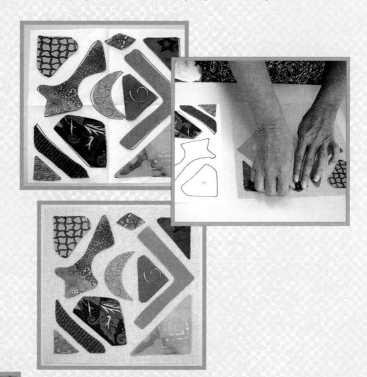

We used a hand-embroidered blanket stitch to appliqué the center shape in each block. The big stitches really make these pieces stand out. You can do all of the shapes this way, or use the sewing machine to appliqué the rest.

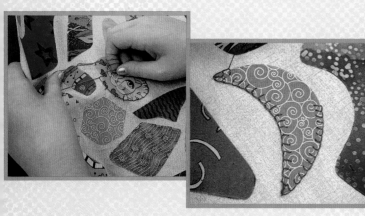

Cut your sashes:

From your sashing fabric, cut six strips 1¼" wide and 24" long. Cut one strip in half to make two shorter pieces.

Join the blocks and sashing strips:

Lay out your blocks in the arrangement you like. Measure your blocks and cut the small strips to fit in between two of them. Pin to hold the edges and use a ¼" seam to sew them together. Do the same with the second pair. Hint! If you join your blocks top to bottom, your center strip will run vertically. Press the seam allowances toward the narrow strips.

Measure both rows of blocks and trim a sashing strip to the right length to join the rows together. When you sew, be sure the short sashings are exactly across from each other and both rows finish the same length. Press the seam allowances toward the narrow strip.

Add sashing strips to the top and bottom of the quilt top. Press the seams toward the narrow strips and trim the corners to make them square if you need to. Sew sashing strips to each side. Press the seams and square the corners again.

Add the borders:

If you have a solid or print border, you can follow the directions in previous projects to add borders with butted corners. We think a striped fabric looks better with mitered corners. Follow these simple steps to add a mitered frame to your quilt:

Cut borders 4½" wide and 32" long. Match the center of a border strip to the center of the top edge of your quilt and sew it with ¼" seam.

Be sure to start and stop your seam ¼" from each corner. Don't sew all the way to the raw edge. Add the other three border strips the same way.

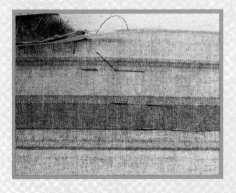

Sew a mitered seam:

Fold the quilt corner to corner, and lay one border strip on top of the other. Make sure the seam lines and corners match.

Put the 45-degree line of your ruler on the border seam and draw a diagonal line on your border strip, as shown.

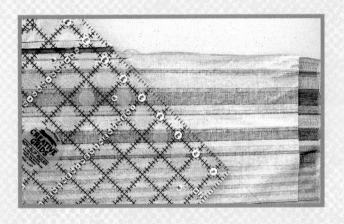

Pin across the sewing line to hold the layers together. Be sure to match the stripes of one border strip to the other border strip.

Start stitching at the exact point your border seams end and sew the miter seam, following the line you drew.

Open the border corner to make sure it is square and the stripes match.

If you are happy with the seam, trim away the extra fabric. Leave a ¼" seam allowance.

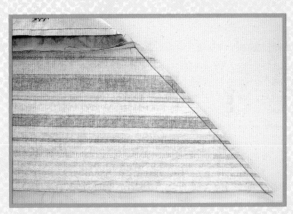

Miter all four corners the same way. Enjoy your striped frame!

Quilt the quilt:

Give your quilt top another good pressing to make sure it is flat and straight. Layer it with batting and backing and baste to hold the layers together. Start the quilting with straight lines in the ditch to frame and stabilize the quilt blocks.

This mosaic quilt was a group project and everyone had a hand at free-motion quilting. It was fun moving the quilt around under the needle. We tried to keep our quilting stitches in the background, so our mosaic pieces would stand up.

Willow

Beverly

Amber

Brandon

Since the striped border is so busy, we decided not to add another pattern on top of it. Quilting the lines of the stripes adds enough texture. If you want to quilt straight lines in your border, use a walking foot to keep the layers even as you work.

Follow the directions for Double Bias Binding on page 64 to bind the quilt.

Mosaic Appliqué in traditional colors made by Anita. Hand appliquéd and hand quilted.

Enlarge pattern 200%

Enlarge pattern 200%

Enlarge pattern 200%

Enlarge pattern 200%

Resources

www.anitashackelford.com
  Anita Shackelford and Jennifer Perdue
  Longarm quilting services
  RucheMark ruching guide
  Infinite Feathers template
  Digitized quilting patterns
  Quilting books, tools, and templates

www.berninausa.com
  domestic sewing machines

www.gammill.net
  longarm quilting machines

www.jbquilter.com
  Mary Eddy, quilting patterns

www.legacyquilting.com
  Todd Brown, digitized quilting patterns

www.mountaintopquilting.com
  Kay Oft, quilting patterns, books, and classes

www.quiltrecipes.com
  Ellen Munnich, digitized quilting designs

www.quiltsavvy.com
  Tonya Del Tongo Armanasco, longarm quilting service, patterns, and classes

www.sharonschamber.com
  Piece-lique book

www.statlerstitcher.com
  Statler Stitcher computerized quilting systems

www.stonevalleyquilting.com
  Deb Kerr, longarm quilting

www.sweetdreamsquiltstudio.com
  Kim Diamond, longarm quilting patterns

www.tkquilting.com
  Tammy Finkler, longarm quilting patterns

www.weebeequilting.com
  Janice Bahrt, longarm quilting services

www.picturetrail.com/dogwoodqlt
  Dogwood Quilting of Baltimore, Marty Vint, longarm quilting services

The Group

Rose Willow Buckelew is 13 years old. She is creative and loves to have fun. She likes music, singing, dancing, and quilting.

Kaitlin Finkler is 18 years old. She enjoys playing her baritone sax and guitar and listening to music.

Samantha Finkler is 13 years old. She likes playing the trumpet and the piano, riding her horse "Mister," and sewing.

Tammy Finkler is a mother, a pattern designer, and an award-winning machine quilter. Along with quilting, she enjoys horses and gardening.

Beverly Morgan is a mother and an avid gardener. She is also a ceramist and multimedia artist who delights in recycling discarded bits and pieces into something new.

Amber Perdue is 15 years old. She plays the clarinet and loves texting, shopping, and hanging out with friends.

Brandon Perdue is 13 years old. He plays the drums and likes to play wrestling and jump on the trampoline with his friends.

Dakota Rapp is 13 years old. He likes to skateboard and play football with friends.

Seayra Spears is 11 years old. She loves music, snowboarding, and swimming.

Blake Zealor is an active 5-year-old who loves monster trucks and motorcycles.

Elisa Shackelford Zealor has done commercial machine embroidery for many years. She has a busy family life and enjoys motorcycles and music.

About the Authors

Jennifer Shackelford Perdue
jen@thimbleworks.com

Jen made her first quilt at age 10 and has continued to enjoy both sewing and quilting. She has a background in garment making, home dec, machine piecing, hand quilting, and longarm quilting. She is currently quilting for others, using a Gammill Optimum with a Statler Stitcher.

Jen's quilts have been included in both regional and national shows and have won awards including several First-Place ribbons, Best Machine Quilting, and Judge's Recognition. She was also awarded Third place in the Young Designers Category at AQS in 2007. Her quilts have been published on the Gammill Web site Showcase Gallery of winning quilts and *American Quilter* magazine. She also made an appearance as part of a quilt group on *Today's American Quilter* television program.

She is a member of the American Quilter's Society and the National Quilting Association.

Jen enjoys an active family life with her husband Scott, and her two children, Amber and Brandon. She also works with a 3-D CAD program, designing custom jewelry.

About the Authors

Anita Shackelford
www.anitashackelford.com

Anita Shackelford has been a quiltmaker since 1967 and began teaching in 1980. She is an internationally recognized teacher and lecturer who loves combining appliqué and fine hand quilting to create new quilts in nineteenth-century style. She also enjoys using her sewing machine for many parts of the creative process and has recently added longarm quilting to the mix.

Anita has been featured on several television programs, including *Today's American Quilter, Kaye's Quilting Friends, Linda's Electric Quilters,* and *Simply Quilts*. Her work and antique quilts from her collection have been featured in several gallery and museum exhibits.

Her quilts have been exhibited in shows across the United States, in Australia, and Japan, winning many award, including twelve Best Of Show and many for workmanship. Two of her quilts have received the Mary Krickbaum Award for best hand quilting at National Quilting Association shows. Her quilts have been published in numerous books and magazines.

Anita is the author of *Three-Dimensional Appliqué and Embroidery Embellishment: Techniques For Today's Album Quilt; Anita Shackelford: Surface Textures; Appliqué with Folded Cutwork; Coxcomb Variations; Infinite Feathers;* and *A Modern Mix,* all published by American Quilter's Society.

Anita has been a member of the National Quilting Association since 1982 and served four years on the NQA Board as membership chair. She is a charter member of the American Quilter's Society and the Museum of American Quilter's Society.

Anita travels extensively, teaching and lecturing for shops, guilds, and quilting conferences. She is a quilt judge, certified by NQA and qualified to judge Masterpiece quilts, and has been involved in judging shows at local, regional, and national levels. She is currently the program coordinator and serves on the faculty for NQA's Quilt Judging Seminar.

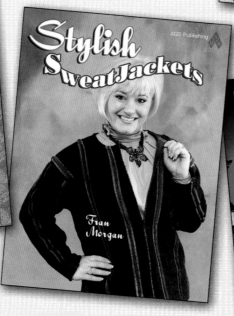